What is European cake?

Au cake is the common name for all kinds of cakes originating from the European region. Most European cakes are made from flour and are baked in an oven. Au cake has a characteristic delicious taste, plus a beautiful and eye-catching appearance, so it is increasingly popular with many people.

It is impossible to know exactly when Au cake appeared in Vietnam. From the French colonial period until the American war broke out, Westerners who came and lived in Vietnam made delicious and scrumptious cakes. Before that, Western cakes were also present at trade meetings, important events of the court, and were an important part of parties.

Some famous European cakes in Vietnam such as: regular bread (Lean yeast bread), sweet bread (Rich yeast bread), quick bread (Quick bread), Donuts (donuts), Pancake, Cake / Gato cake, Crepe...

Cakes Can Reduce Stress

The aroma of baked goods and cakes is a medicine that helps reduce stress and has a calming effect on nerves. According to the results of research by scientists on human psychology, the fat in cakes helps stimulate the brain to release more endorphins and seretonins, thereby bringing an indescribable euphoria and happy mood for people, baker and connoisseur.

Do Cakes Make You Smarter?

According to neuroscientist Alan Hirsch, several studies have shown that cakes help stimulate beta waves in the brain and have a stimulating effect on alertness.

Also according to another study, people who do heavy mental or mental work after being allowed to smell the aroma of the cake will become very intelligent, alert, more lucid and complete the work quickly, more than the others.

Donuts

Ingredients for making Donuts with an oil-free fryer

- All-purpose flour 350 gr
- Dried yeast 6.5 gr
- Powdered sugar 250 gr
- Sugar 86 gr
- Fresh milk without sugar 120 ml
- Chicken eggs 2
- Unsalted butter 60 ml
- Vanilla essence 2 tablespoons
- Corn syrup 1 tbsp
- Salt 1/2 teaspoon
- Cooking oil 10 ml
- Warm water 120 ml

What is all-purpose flour?

All-purpose flour, also known as flour number 11, is an ingredient commonly used in baking recipes.

Currently, all-purpose flour includes two main types: bleached and unbleached. Bleached flour is a powder that has had its inherent yellow pigment removed, suitable for making bread or cakes.

Flour is one of the most important ingredients in baking. Because it helps create texture and firmness for cakes.

You can easily find and buy flour at food stores, supermarkets, grocery stores, markets, bakeries, and reputable e-commerce sites in the market like Bach Khoa XANH to make sure. food safety and hygiene.

What is dry yeast?

Dry yeast is one of the types of yeast (Yeast), with the coarse, large brown seeds used to increase the baking powder, spongy and capable of secreting substances to help the dough ferment faster.

To use dry yeast, you need to activate the yeast first by soaking it in warm water and then mixing that quality part with the cake flour.

Implementation tools

Oil-free fryer, kneading machine, bowl, cage stirrer, flattener, mold,...

How to cook Donuts with an oil-free fryer

1.Activate yeast

First, you put 120ml of warm water mixed with 60ml of warm unsweetened fresh milk into a measuring cup or cup.

Then, add about 6.5g of dry yeast and 21g of granulated sugar to the milk mixture, stir well with a spatula and let the yeast rest for about 5-10 minutes.

Note:

The milk temperature to activate yeast will range from 32 - 38 degrees Celsius (no more than 40 degrees Celsius), not hotter because it will kill the yeast or weaken its activity.

If you're using instant yeast, you can add it directly into the flour mixture.

2.Mixing and tempering the dough
You put the ingredients in the dough mixer: 60ml melted butter, 65g granulated sugar, 1 egg, 1 egg yolk, 1 teaspoon vanilla essence, 1/2 teaspoon salt and 310g flour multi-use. Finally, pour all the dry yeast mixture into the dough bowl.

Next, you turn on the machine at low speed to mix and knead the dough for about 5-7 minutes, then slowly increase the speed of the machine to mix for another 5 minutes until it forms a fixed dough, the dough does not stick to the wall. mixing bowl is okay!

Outward remittance:

If you don't have a kneading machine, you can knead by hand using the Folding and Stretching technique. First, you fold the dough, then use the back of the table to press and spread the dough away.
With this technique, it is important to press and spread the dough away, not down. Next rotate the dough at an angle of 90 degrees and then repeat the two steps above for 15-20 minutes.
When baking the dough, you should put the bowl of dough in the oven, so the dough will rise more evenly and puff more!

3. Roll the dough and shape the cake
First, sprinkle some flour on the table, take the dough out of the bowl and sprinkle some more flour on top of the cake.

Next, use a rolling pin to roll out the dough to a thickness of about 1/2 small.

Next, you use a round mold to press firmly on the surface of the dough, turn it slightly so that the mold evenly cuts the dough.

Then, place a smaller round mold in the center of the large circle, pressing the mold down. Repeat this until the surface of the dough is covered.

Next, you slowly tear the excess dough around the large circle and separate the small circle, put the large circle and the small circle on a tray (lined with wax paper).

As for the remaining dough, you knead it together and then roll it out and cut the cake like at the beginning. Finally, you continue to rest the dough for about 20-30 minutes before putting it in the air fryer.

4.Fry cake
Preheat the air fryer at 180 degrees Celsius for 3 minutes. Then, spread a thin layer of cooking oil around the inside of the pot and put in each cake in turn, avoiding the cakes close to each other, but should create a space for the cakes to puff up after frying.

Lower the pot temperature to about 160 degrees Celsius and fry the cakes for about 5-6 minutes, open the inner pot and leave the cakes in the pot for about 2 minutes, then take them out.

As for the small round cake, you also fry it for 5-6 minutes cook until the cake is golden.

5.Make sugar coating
To make the sugar coating, put 250g of powdered sugar and 60ml of fresh milk in a bowl, add 1 tablespoon corn syrup, 1 tablespoon vanilla essence. Then, use a spatula to mix the mixture until it becomes a thick, thick mixture, without any more dough.

Finally, dip one side of the cake into the sugar coating and place it on a tray with a rack. For small cakes, you put in a bowl of sugar, mix well and then use a fork to remove the cake from the tray and you're done.

6.Finished product
Donuts are fried in an oil-free fryer until golden, fragrant with beautiful circles. Biting a piece of cake, you will feel the softness and light sponginess of the cake flour mixed with the sweet and greasy layer of sugar. Let's try it now!

Chiffon

Material

- 2 industrial chicken eggs
- 25g corn flour
- 25g all-purpose flour
- 30g fresh milk without sugar
- 25g cooking oil
- 2 drops of vanilla
- Little salt
- 1/2 tsp lemon juice
- 40g sugar

Step 1: Separate the whites and yolks in 2 bowls (clean bowl, no water or fat, white without yolk)

Step 2: Add 25g cornstarch, 25g flour, 30g fresh milk, 25g cooking oil -> mix well and add vanilla (the mixture is not thick, not liquid and flowing continuously)

Step 3: Add the whites for salt, lemon juice -> beat -> foam like soap -> slowly add 40g of sugar to the end -> increase the speed of the machine to the highest and beat until the peak is vertical and slightly Turn it down, face down, don't fall

Step 4: Turn on the pot 180 degrees before 2 minutes to bake the cake with an air fryer

Step 5: Divide the whites into 3 parts. Place each portion into the bowl of yolks and fold the dough evenly. If you are not confident, take a folding spatula to make sure! Just do it definitely, mix a lot and break all the air bubbles and the cake will be flat

Step 6: Pour the dough into the mold. Lightly tap the mold to break up large air bubbles for a smooth texture. Put the cake in the pot, bake the cake in an oil-free fryer at 155 degrees for 25 minutes.

Test the cake with a skewer, if the toothpick comes out dry, the cake is done. Take out the cake and drop it on the table 2-3 from a height of 20-30cm -> turn the cake upside down on a rack to wait for it to cool, then take a knife to peel the cake and take out the cake.

An international student who lacks all kinds of tools can still make soft, fragrant, and elastic egg-oiled sponge cakes ^^! As long as you know the recipe for making the cake base and the notes, it will be successful even if you make the cake with an oil-free fryer or an electric rice cooker.

Croissant
Croissant

Materials

- 5 g of yeast
- 250 g flour number 13
- 35 g sugar (customized to taste)
- 70g warm water
- 70g unsweetened milk
- 5g salt
- 1 egg
- 20 g melted butter
- 120g soft butter

How to make croissants

Create dough blocks

Put the salted sugar powder in the same bowl and mix well (1)
In another bowl, mix the water + milk + yeast + eggs
Pour the mixture and begin to knead the dough. The powder
doesn't need to be too fine, just absorb the liquid.
Cover the dough and put it in the fridge for 30 minutes and then
knead until smooth.

Roll the dough out to a size of about 25×25 cm, this part is okay if
the dough shrinks a bit. Cover with a towel and cling film to keep
the cake moist. Incubate in the refrigerator for 1-12 hours (the
longer the cake, the better)

Cut wax paper to spread 120 g butter 20×10 cm size. Spread the butter with a rolling pin, roll the butter to the corners and refrigerate it for the same amount of time as the dough has risen. Stencils for folding dough

When cutting you should cut 1-2 cm more to make sure the butter is completely covered and pay attention to the corners when

Fold (Fold the dough)

To get a "thousand layer" cake, you need to "fold" the cake 3 times, all using the "threefolds" technique. After 1 and 2 turn the dough 90 degrees (right fold) and roll out another 31×10 cm. Between each "fold" should put the dough in the freezer for 30 minutes so that the butter does not melt. Note: Please work quickly.

After 3 times of "folding", continue to put the dough in the refrigerator for 1-8 hours. This is when the ingredients "work" together to create the best cake. So just patiently waiting for the cake will be more delicious.

Shaping croissants

Take the dough out of the refrigerator, roll the dough 28×20 cm
Trim excess edges for a square dough, which will usually reduce the width of the dough by 1 cm.
Measure and cut the dough into 7 equal triangles.
Stretch the triangle out about 2 cm, rol

Chocolate Cake

Prepare materials

- 1. All-purpose flour 63g
- 2. Cocoa powder 21g
- 3. Baking powder ¼ teaspoon
- 4. Baking soda ¼ teaspoon
- 5. Salt 1/8 teaspoon
- 6. Egg 1 large egg
- 7. Vegetable oil 60ml
- 8. Buttermilk 60ml
- 9. Vanilla essence 1 teaspoon
- 10. Sugar 133g
- 11. Hot water 45ml

This air fryer-baked chocolate cake has a moist, soft texture and is exceptionally easy to make. This is the recipe for a small chocolate cake with a size of 15cm, the size of a regular air fryer. This recipe is perfect for small families who don't want to bake a large cake. You can enjoy the chocolate cake with a cup of coffee or topped with a layer of chocolate cream before serving.

How to make chocolate cake with air fryer

1.Prepare the cake mold
Prepare a piece of foil according to the diameter of the mold. Place a damp paper towel along the length of the foil.

Close up. Then roll this piece into the center of the mold.

Outside, wrap an extra layer of foil around the mold.

Line the bottom and sides of the mold with parchment paper. Heat the air fryer to 160 degrees Celsius.

2.Prepare the cake dough
In a large bowl, whisk together flour, cocoa powder, baking powder, baking soda and salt and set aside.

In another large mixing bowl, whisk together eggs, oil, buttermilk, and vanilla. Add sugar and beat until frothy for 1 minute.

Add flour mixture and mix until evenly combined. At this point add hot water gradually. Just add and mix well, will help the dough thinner.

Pour the dough into the prepared cake pan.

3.Preparing for baking
Use foil to cover the top of the cake pan. Poke a few small holes in the top of the foil to allow steam to escape while baking.

Bake for 45 minutes, then remove the foil and bake for an additional 5 minutes if needed.

Use a toothpick to skewer the cake and when it comes out clean, the cake is done. Let the cake rest in the pan to cool for about 15 minutes.

Then remove the cake from the mold, transfer to a cooling rack and let cool completely.

You can decorate the cake to your liking or use it right away. Cakes will be soft and moist for up to 4 days when stored in an airtight container at room temperature. If you are filling or decorating ice cream, it cannot be stored at room temperature. You can keep the cake in an airtight container in the refrigerator for up to 5 days.

Macaron Cake

Macaron Cake Ingredients

- 300g powdered sugar
- 70g almond powder
- Food coloring
- 2 chicken eggs
- Street

How to make Macarons

Step 1 Sift flour
Mix 2 types including 300g of powdered sugar and 70g of almond flour together, then use a stainless steel mesh racket to sift the above powder.

Step 2 Beat egg whites
Put 2 egg whites in a bowl and use a whisk to beat until the egg whites are opaque, add 30 grams of sugar about 2 times in turn and beat for about 3 more minutes. You beat the eggs until the whites are smooth, tilt the bowl without spilling.

Step 3 Mix flour with egg whites
Put the flour mixture with the beaten egg whites in a bowl, mix well, until the mixture is smooth and no longer pitted.

Then, use food coloring mixed with flour to make the cake more beautiful.

Step 4 Shape the cake and bake it with the air fryer

Put the powder mixed with food coloring into the puff pastry bag and then shape the tray into just the right size. You can add a purple cake to decorate the top of the cake.

When shaping is complete, leave the cake at room temperature for about 40 minutes until the surface is dry, then it can be baked.

Put the cake into the pot and turn the fryer temperature to 165 degrees Celsius, bake for about 20 minutes.

3 Finished Products

Macaron cake is delicious and beautiful when tasted, sweet and fatty. The cake is soft, with a characteristic almond aroma. Sipping a delicious Macaron cake with a cup of hot tea, chatting with relatives and friends is a great choice.

Cheese Corn Muffins

Ingredients to be prepared

- 60 gr all-purpose flour
- 79 gr corn flour
- 38 gr white sugar
- 6 gr salt
- 7 gr baking powder (baking soda)
- 118 ml of fresh milk
- 45 gr butter, melted
- 1 egg
- 165 grams of corn
- 3 sprigs of scallions, chopped
- 120 gr cheddar cheese, finely grated
- Oil spray bottle

Make Cheese Corn Muffins

Step 1: Mix flour, cornstarch, sugar, salt and baking powder in a large bowl.

Step 2: In another bowl, whisk together the milk, butter, and eggs. Gently mix the dry mixture into the bowl of the wet mixture. Gently toss corn, scallions, and grated cheddar cheese.

Step 3: Select the mode Preheat the Cosori Air Fryer at 160°C and press Start.

Step 4: Spray cooking oil on muffin molds to prevent sticking and pour in flour no more than 3/4. Place the muffin pan in the preheated frying basket.

Step 5: Select Bread mode, adjust time 15 minutes and press Start. Enjoy the cake with butter or eat it right away.

Chrysanthemum Bread

Ingredients for making chrysanthemum bread

- All-purpose flour 230 gr
- Instant yeast 5 gr
- Chicken eggs 2
- Fresh milk without sugar 60 ml
- Unsalted Butter 80 gr
- Almonds 1 piece (slice type)
- Neroli essential oil 2.5 ml
- Sugar/salt 1 pinch

Implementation tools

Air fryer, bowl, stencils, spoon, food wrap,...

How to make Chrysanthemum Bread

1.Stimulating yeast bloom
First, you prepare a cup for 5g of yeast, 200ml of warm water from 32 - 38 degrees Celsius. Add 20g of sugar to the yeast and water mixture and stir until dissolved.

Leave for about 15 minutes until the glaze floats like crab bricks.

2.Mix cake dough
Add 230g all-purpose flour, 1/4 teaspoon salt, 40g sugar, 1 egg, yeast mixture, 2.5ml neroli essential oil, 80g unsalted butter and 60ml unsweetened fresh milk and mix well. .

3. Kneading the dough

Knead the dough with your hands until it is sticky. Then start kneading according to the Folding and Strectching technique.

First, you fold the dough, then use the back of your hand to press and spread the dough away. Note that pressing and spreading the dough away, not down. Next rotate the dough at a 90 degree angle and then repeat the two steps over 10 minutes.

When the dough begins to smooth, add 30g of unsalted butter, then repeat the above kneading for another 15 minutes until the dough forms a uniform, smooth, elastic mass.

4.Incubate the dough

Cover the bowl with cling film or thin cloth and let the dough rise for about 45 minutes, depending on room temperature, until the dough has doubled in size.

5.Create a chrysanthemum shape

Divide the dough into 4 equal parts, roll each piece into a piece about 30cm long and braid.

Incubate the dough for the second time, put the dough into the mold, cover the surface of the mold with food wrap, incubate the dough for about 20 minutes in a warm place until the dough has doubled in size compared to when it was put in the mold.

After the dough has been incubated for the second time, so that the cake after baking has a beautiful golden brown color, use a brush to gently brush the leftover beaten egg on the surface of the cake. Then sprinkle the sliced almonds evenly.

6.Baking cake
First, you must preheat the air fryer at 160 degrees for about 4 minutes.

Next, you put the cake into the pot tray, then bake the cake at about 160 degrees Celsius for 5 minutes, then you open the pot, turn the cake and bake for about 5 more minutes for the cake to cook evenly.

7.Finished product
The chrysanthemum bread is sweet, soft, delicious, greasy with a rich, characteristic butter aroma. The bread is thoroughly baked, so it has a very eye-catching golden color.

This cake is very suitable for family breakfast. You can use the cake with tea or fresh milk.

Cupcakes

Ingredients for making cupcakes

- All-purpose flour 200 gr
- Cornstarch 100 gr
- Vanilla powder 1 tube
- Chicken eggs 6 eggs
- Fresh milk without sugar 40 ml
- 1/2 lemon
- Cooking oil 40 ml (can use butter instead)
- Powdered sugar 100 gr
- Salt 1/3 teaspoon

Implementation tools
Oil-free fryer, stirrer, bowl, strainer, spoon,...

How to make Cupcakes

1. Beat egg yolk mixture
First, separate the egg whites and egg yolks into 2 different bowls. Next, use a whisk to beat the egg yolks until fluffy, then add 40ml of unsweetened fresh milk and 30ml of cooking oil.

Just add slowly and continue to beat until the mixture is fluffy, add 1 tube of vanilla powder, so the cake will not have a fishy egg smell. If you don't have vanilla powder, you can also use the liquid form.

Then, using a sieve, slowly sift all the cornstarch and prepared flour into the beaten egg yolk mixture, use a patch to mix well from the outside to the inside until the egg powder mixture is smooth. Then set aside to let the dough rest for 15-20 minutes.

2. Whip the egg whites
Next, we will use a whisk to beat the egg whites. Then, squeeze the juice of 1/2 lemon into a bowl of beaten egg whites with 1/3 teaspoon of salt.

Continue to beat until the mixture is about 5 minutes to slightly fluffy, then divide 100g of powdered sugar into 3 parts and add sugar slowly. Mix and beat for about 10 more minutes, until the eggs have peaks and turn the bowl upside down without spilling.

3.Mix the cake flour mixture
Slowly add the flour and egg yolk mixture to the beaten egg whites. Use a patch to mix from the outside to the inside very gently so that the air bubbles do not break until the two mixtures are blended and smooth.

4. Bake cupcakes in an oil-free fryer
Prepare a baking pan and then apply a layer of oil or butter evenly to the mold to make it easier to remove the cake. Then scoop each piece of beaten egg powder into the mold.

Finally, put the cake molds in an oil-free fryer and bake at 160 degrees Celsius for 10 minutes until the cakes are golden brown.

5.Finished product
So you have completed the cupcake with a super simple oil-free fryer right at home.

The cupcake has a beautiful golden brown color, the cake is soft, has a moderate sweet taste, mixed with the passionate aroma of delicious custard, you will surely love it.

Tiramisu

Ingredients to be prepared

- 100g flour number 11
- 10g cocoa powder
- 50g cake sugar water
- 6g cooking oil
- 5g peanut butter
- 50 gr of coffee flavored mooncake slug
- 15g cream cheese
- Egg yolk
- Moon cake mold

Make tiramisu with an oil-free fryer

Step 1: Put the flour and cocoa powder in a bowl, mix well and make a hole in the bottom of the bowl.

Step 2: Put baking soda, cooking oil and peanut butter into that hole. Mix well, knead gently until dough is smooth and even. Let the dough rest for 40 minutes.

Step 3: Take a little bit of coffee cake, press it flat, put cream cheese in the middle and then round it.

Step 4: Take a little dough to press flat, continue to round around the cake.

Step 5: Turn on the Heat mode on the Cosori Air Fryer

Step 6: Put the rounded cake into the cake mold and shape it.

Step 7: Brush a layer of egg yolk on the surface of the cake. Place the cake in the preheated frying basket.

Step 8: Set 160 degrees Celsius within 7 minutes for the first time. Continue setting 150 degrees Celsius for 5 minutes for the 2nd time.

Let cool and enjoy right away.

You can store it in an airtight container for up to 5 days.

Pateso

Ingredients for making pateso with an oil-free fryer

- Flour milled cake 500 gr
- Minced pork 300 gr
- Pate 150 gr
- Margarine 1 tablespoon
- Onion 200 gr
- Egg yolk 1 pc
- Fresh milk without sugar 1 tbsp
- Oyster oil 1 tbsp
- Common seasoning 1 little

(seasoning/monosodium glutamate/sugar)

What is thousand-layer powder? Where to buy ready-made thousand-layer flour?

Thousand-layer dough, also known as Puff Pastry - this is a type of dough that, after baking, will expand and form many overlapping layers.
You can buy thousand-layer flour at baking supply stores, large supermarkets or online on e-commerce sites.
How to choose and buy fresh ingredients

How to choose clean, safe pork?

Pork should choose the meat with bright pink color, pink white skin. Choose the meat with the right amount of fat, the outer skin is thin, the pressed meat has a certain elasticity and has a specific smell.

Should not choose meat parts that are dark or pale green, when pressed, the meat is soft and has no elasticity.

Do not buy meat that has too much fat, the outer layer of skin is thick and hard, and has a bad smell. Because they may have been left for too long or are aged pork, they will no longer taste good. You can buy ready-made minced pork from the market and process it, but it will be difficult to check the quality of the meat. It is best to buy whole pork and mince it yourself or grind it with a meat grinder to ensure safety and quality when using.
See details: How to choose to buy fresh, quality pork
How to choose and buy good, quality pate

A good pate is a brown pate, soft and smooth, neither too dry nor too hard.
In addition, should buy pate when smelling no strange smell or appearing moldy stains on the surface because it is pate that has been left for a long time, eating will have a bad effect on health.

See more:

What is pate?
How to make pork liver pate with greasy, delicious pork
Ingredients for pateso dishes in an oil-free fryer

Implementation tools
Air fryer, bowl, spoon, knife, fork,...

How to cook pateso in an oil-free fryer

1.Meat filling
First, put in a bowl 300g minced pork, 200g diced onion, 1 tbsp seasoning, 1/2 tbsp MSG, 2 tbsp sugar, 1 tbsp oyster sauce.

Then, stir the mixture until the meat absorbs the spices and the ingredients blend together.

Next, you add 150gr pate, 1 tablespoon margarine in a bowl and continue to mix until the ingredients are evenly mixed.

2.Make the cake spread
In a new bowl, add 1 egg yolk, 1 tablespoon of unsweetened fresh milk and stir well.

3. Shape the cake
Use a round mold to cut the dough into 6 equal pieces.

Next, put about 1 tablespoon of filling in the center of the dough, place another piece of dough on top and press firmly around the edges of the dough to stick together.

Next, use a fork to gently press around the edges of the dough again to make the cake stick better.

4.Baking cake

Preheat the air fryer to 200 degrees Celsius for 5 minutes.

Next, spread a layer of egg mixture on the top of the cake, this step will help the cake have a more beautiful color, then put the cake in an air fryer to bake at 180 degrees Celsius for 15 minutes.

5.Finished product

The finished pateso cake made with an oil-free fryer has a crispy, fragrant, fatty crust mixed with a rich meat filling that is both delicious and extremely nutritious!

Empanadas

Material

- Wrapper
- Wheat flour
- Country
- Salt
- Pork fat won the water
- Cake filling
- Minced beef or minced pork depending on preference
- Chopped bell peppers
- Minced Onion
- Dried chili if you like spicy food
- Boiled chicken eggs
- Salt
- Black pepper

Finishing Empanadas with an Air Fryer

With the help of an oil-free fryer, Empanadas come out of the oven not only delicious, but also limit up to 80% of the harmful fats produced during frying. The steps are as follows:

Making pie crust

Put salt in a pot of lard, bring to a gentle boil on the stove, stir well, then add the flour. Continue to mix, knead until the dough becomes very smooth, then stop. Store in the fridge for about 2 hours.

Take the dough out, roll it to about 3mm thin.
Shaped like a round ball ready to be filled

Making the cake

Beef / Pork brought to hunt, seasoned with spices
Bell peppers, onions are mixed with oil, add paprika, salt, pepper, ...
stir well.
Boiled eggs, peeled, cut into small pieces, then add the meat, the
mixture of bell peppers, onions, and mix all the ingredients.
How to make Empanadas with an oil-free fryer
How to make Empanadas with an oil-free fryer – Photo: Internet

Fry Empanadas in an oil-free fryer
After having the crust and filling, begin to perfect the cake
sequentially as follows:

Put the filling in the middle of the cake, fold the dough in half to
form a beautiful semicircle.
Place the cake in an oil-free fryer, fry for 20 minutes, at a
temperature of 180 degrees Celsius. When the cake turns golden,
the cake is ready.
Arrange on a plate.

Korean Black Sesame Bread

Ingredients for Korean Black Sesame Bread

- All-purpose flour 30 gr
- Tapioca flour 150 gr
- Black sesame 25 gr
- Chicken eggs 2
- Unsalted butter 30 gr
- Fresh milk without sugar 150 ml
- Milk powder 20 gr
- Sugar 30 gr

Implementation tools
Air fryer, pot, bowl, fork, spoon, stencil,...

How to make Korean Black Sesame Bread

1.Cook the flour mixture
Put the pot on the stove on medium heat, put in the pot 30g unsalted butter, 150ml fresh milk, 20g milk powder, 30g sugar, gently stir with a whisk.

Then sift 30g flour into the pot, adjust the heat to low, gently stir with a spatula for 3-4 minutes until the dough thickens, then turn off the heat.

2.Mix the dough
When the dough in the pot is still hot, add 150g of tapioca starch

(divided into 3 times), use a spatula to stir until the dough mixture forms a homogeneous mass.

Next, you add to the flour mixture 2 eggs, 25g of black sesame, then mix well, put the mixture in an ice cream bag.

3.Baking cake
To stabilize the fryer, open the pot first at 200 degrees Celsius for 3 minutes.

You prepare a frying tray lined with parchment paper, pump the cake mixture up, then put the tray into the fryer, bake the first time at a temperature of 175 degrees C for 10 minutes.

When enough time is up, open the fryer, turn the cake over and bake it a second time at 175 degrees Celsius for 5 minutes to complete.

4.Finished product
So the delicious crispy Korean black sesame bread is finished, the crust is crispy, fragrant, the black sesame is juicy, and the sweetness is just right, so anyone who tries it will surely fall in love.

Apple Pie

Ingredients for making apple pie with an oil-free fryer

- 1 apple
- All-purpose flour 200 g
- Baking powder 5 g
- Chicken eggs 2
- Sugar 150 g
- Milk 100 ml
- Butter 30 g

How to choose good apples

Should choose apples with glossy skin, fresh colors, no rough feeling when touched. If you like to eat sweet apples, you can choose the dark ones with tiny white seeds.
Do not choose apples that are dull, crushed, or damaged.
Ingredients for upside down apple pie dish in an oil-free fryer

Implementation tools
Oil-free fryer, bowl, mixer

How to cook upside down apple pie in an air fryer

1.Cooking Caramel
Put in the pot 15g butter, 1 tablespoon sugar, 15ml water, stir over medium heat until the mixture turns brown, then turn off the heat.

2.Cut and arrange apples in the mold
Wash apples, remove seeds and stems and cut into thin slices.

Line the parchment paper, alternately arrange the apples in the mold, then drizzle the caramel evenly over the apple.

3.Mix cake dough
Put in a bowl 200g flour, 5g baking powder, 15g butter, 2 eggs, 135g sugar, 100ml fresh milk. Stir until the mixture is combined and smooth.

Note: The sugar you can add or reduce according to your sweet taste.
4.Baking cake
Pour the cake batter into the mold.

Preheat the air fryer at 180 degrees Celsius for 10 minutes, then bake the cakes at 135 degrees for 25 minutes.

5.Finished product
Apple cake upside down is fragrant thanks to avocado camramel, the apple piece is crispy, sweet, served with a layer of fluffy, soft sponge cake, just try one and you will love it!

Cream Puff Pastry

Ingredients for making cream puff pastry

- Fresh milk without sugar 240 ml (for pie crust)
- Household flour 75 gr (for pie crust)
- Sugar 1 teaspoon (for pie crust)
- 2 eggs (for pie crust)
- Butter 100 gr (for pie crust)
- Salt 1/4 teaspoon (for pie crust)
- Cornstarch 20 gr (for the filling)
- 4 eggs (for the filling)
- Sugar 60 gr (for the filling)
- Fresh milk without sugar 300 ml (for the filling)

Ingredients for cream puff pastry

Implementation tools
Oil-free fryer, pot, whisk...

How to make cream puff pastry

1.Make the crust
First, to prevent the dough from becoming lumpy, we will sift the flour into a large bowl, so that the cake is smoother.

Take a pot, put in 240ml of unsweetened fresh milk, 100g of butter, 1 teaspoon of sugar, 1/4 teaspoon of salt, 1 teaspoon of vanilla and cook on low heat until the mixture boils and the butter melts.

After the above mixture boils, add the flour and mix well, until the dough is flexible and does not stick to the pot, then turn off the heat.

After turning off the stove, you put in the mixture on 2 eggs, add each egg in turn and mix the mixture well.

When the mixture is even, line small pieces of parchment paper or non-stick paper on the griddle of the air fryer. Then put the mixture into an ice cream bag with a large star tip and shape it into small cones on top of the sheets of paper.

Note:
You have to wait for the dough to cool before you add the eggs, if you put the eggs in when the dough is hot, the flour will make the eggs cooked and damage the dough.
Do not squeeze the ice cream too big because the cake will still expand.

2.Baking the crust
When the dough is finished, you can put it in an oil-free fryer and bake for 15-20 minutes at 170 degrees.

After 15-20 minutes, when you pull it out, you can see that the cake is large, golden brown in color, the surface seems to be hard, then the cake is done, then take it out and let it cool on a rack. If you find that the cake is not good, you can fry it for another 5-10 minutes at 160 degrees and then take it out to check.

3.Make the cake
Put in a bowl 4 egg yolks with 60g sugar, 30g cornstarch and mix well.

Then pour in 300ml of fresh milk and stir again.

Next, pour the above mixture through a sieve into a pot.

Then stir and cook this mixture on medium heat, until the mixture thickens, then turn off the heat.

After the filling is done, leave it for 5 minutes at normal outside temperature and then put it in the refrigerator.

4.Put the filling into the crust
When the cake is done and completely cooled, cut a small line in the middle of the cake body or poke a small hole in the bottom of the cake.

Take out the cake that has been cooked in the refrigerator, put it in an ice cream bag and then squeeze it to fill the inside of the cake.

5.Finished product
After the completion of the cream puff pastry, the crunchiness of the cake's crust and the smooth pastry filling is very attractive. You can use these plates of cream puffs as desserts, as a snack when you're sad, or with tea to talk to your friends.

Notes when making banh chung with an oil-free fryer:

When making the pie crust, squeeze the egg into the dough one at a time or be more careful you can beat 2 eggs in another bowl, then slowly pour in the flour mixture and beat until all are gone. egg. If you put the eggs in at once, it will cause a doughy dough and the cake will not swell, making the cake both bad and not good.

In the first 10 minutes, absolutely do not open the air fryer to see the cake, this will make the cake not yet cooked, but push the air out, which will make the cake not puffy. If you are afraid that the cake will burn, wait for 10 minutes and then open it to see, if it is not cooked, you can lower it 5 degrees for 1 time to bake again for 5-10 minutes.

Tips for preserving cream puffs:
After making the cake, put it in an airtight container and put it in the refrigerator for 2 days or you can keep the crust and the filling separately, when you eat, squeeze the filling into the cake. However, you should only keep the cake for a maximum of 1 day because the cake will dry out and lose its delicious taste.

Baked Banana Cake

Ingredients for Baked Banana Cake

- 2 bananas
- All-purpose flour 4 tablespoons
- 1 chicken egg
- Condensed milk 1 tbsp
- 1 little cooking oil
- Topping 1 little

(dried nuts or dried fruit of your choice)

Where to buy flour?

Currently, you can easily find and buy flour at grocery stores, bakeries, supermarkets or at Bach Khoa XANH supermarket system.

In addition, you can also order at e-commerce sites or buy flour at bachhoaxanh.com website.

See more: What is all-purpose flour? Where to buy all-purpose flour and how to store it?

Ingredients for banana cake baked in an oil-free fryer

Implementation tools

Air fryer, bowl, spoon, chopsticks, stirrer,...

How to make Baked Banana Cake with All-Purpose Flour

1.Mix the dough with banana

Buy bananas, peel off the skins and put them in a bowl and puree the bananas. Next, put 4 tablespoons of flour in a bowl and mix well.

Then crack another egg into the bowl, stir well, add 1 tablespoon of condensed milk and use chopsticks or a whisk to mix well until the mixture is smooth, without lumps.

Finally, add a little raisin topping or any dry fruit, dried seeds according to your preference to complete the cake dough.

2.Baking cake
Put a little cooking oil into the cake pan, spread evenly and add the prepared banana flour mixture.

My air fryer preheated to 180 degrees for 5 minutes. Then add the cake mixture and bake at 160 degrees C for 25 - 30 minutes.

Check the cake is done by inserting a toothpick into the cake, if the cake does not stick to the toothpick, your cake is done and can be removed to enjoy!

3.Finished product
Banana cake has an eye-catching yellow color, very fragrant smell of bananas. The cake is flexible, soft, moderately sweet, with a mild sour and sour topping to increase the deliciousness of the cake. Have a good time!

Buffalo Horn Shrimp Rolls

Ingredients for making buffalo horn shrimp rolls with an oil-free fryer

- Cresent roll powder 220 (1 box)
- Big shrimp 16
- Asparagus 16 plants
- Egg yolk 1 pc

How to choose good shrimp

Delicious fresh shrimp legs will be transparent and stick to the shrimp body. Do not buy shrimp with loose, discolored legs.
Pay attention to buy shrimp with a slightly curved body, firm flesh, intact shrimp shell and shrimp head sticking to the body.
Do not buy shrimp with tail spread, loose, missing caudal fins and not neatly folded together. Maybe shrimp caught a long time ago, soaked through preservatives.
Ingredients for buffalo horn shrimp rolls in an oil-free fryer

Implementation tools
Fryer without oil, knife, cutting board

How to make buffalo horn shrimp rolls with an oil-free fryer

1.Preliminary shrimp processing
Shrimp peel off the tail, remove the back, wash with vinegar, then rinse with water and dry.

Next, you mix shrimp with 1/2 teaspoon seasoning, 1/2 teaspoon pepper.

2.Shrimp roll

With a packet of dough, you will separate 8 pieces, each piece you will cut into 2 small pieces.

Place shrimp and asparagus on top of dough, then roll up.

3.Baking cake

Preheat the air fryer at 165 degrees Celsius for 5 minutes, put the cakes in the oven for 4 minutes.

After 4 minutes, beat the egg yolks and then brush on the cake, continue to bake for another 4 minutes.

4.Finished product

Buffalo horn shrimp rolls have a soft and chewy crust, and the shrimp inside is rich, with the flavor of asparagus. Come to the kitchen to make and taste it, you will surely fall in love with it!

Bread Rolls With Cold Meat

Ingredients for making Bread rolls with cold meat in an oil-free fryer

- All-purpose flour 250 gr
- 1 chicken egg
- Sugar 20 gr
- Salt 1/5 teaspoon
- Instant yeast 2 gr
- Bacon 200 gr
- Cheese 6 slices
- Green onion 1 plant
- Fresh milk without sugar 75 ml
- Fresh cream 75 ml (whipping cream)

Implementation tools
Fryer without oil, stencils

How to cook cold meat rolls in an oil-free fryer

1.Mix the dough
Put in a large bowl or bowl 75ml unsweetened fresh milk, 75ml whipping cream, 1 egg, 20g sugar, 1/5 teaspoon salt, sift 250g all-purpose flour, mix well.

Add 2g instant yeast to the flour mixture, continue to mix until the dough is even.

Note about yeast:

Put the salt and yeast at a distance from each other, if the yeast comes into direct contact with the salt, the yeast will die.

Tips to check if yeast is still active or not: If yeast is not stored properly, it may weaken or die, to check if your yeast is still active or not, put it in a cup of warm water. . After about 5 minutes, when you see the enamel bubbling up a lot on the surface of the water, your yeast is still good to use.

2. Knead the bread dough
You take the dough out onto a clean flat surface.

First you fold the dough, then use the back of your hand, press and rub, push the dough away (Folding and Stretching). Note that pressing and spreading the dough away, not down. Rotate the dough 90 degrees, repeat the two steps above.

Knead until the dough is smooth, the dough does not stick to your hands anymore.

Small tips:

If the dough is a bit dry, you can slowly add a little unsweetened fresh milk!

3.Incubate the dough
Then, you cover the dough, let it rest for about 1 hour, until the dough doubles depending on room temperature.

4.Rolling and rolling meat
After the dough is rested, take out the dough, press it to flatten and then put it on a clean flat surface, use a pestle to roll the dough to about 3mm thin as shown.

Then, you put 200g of bacon on the dough, put 6 slices of cheese on top, cut 1 green onion and sprinkle it on the cake as shown.

Next, you slowly gently roll the cake into a roll as shown. Then use a knife or scissors to cut into small pieces.

Small tips:

You roll the cake tightly so that the cake does not fall apart after cutting!

5.Baking bread
You put the cake in an oil-free fryer tray lined with foil or non-stick parchment paper.

Bake for about 1 hour before baking. Then spread some fresh milk on the cake, cover with foil and bake at 150 degrees Celsius for about 20 minutes.

Then remove the foil, bake for another 15 minutes at 140 degrees Celsius, the cake is completely cooked.

6.Finished product

Bread rolls with cold meat in an air fryer are delicious with soft bread, fragrant cold meat with the fatty taste of cheese, isn't it? Enjoy now!

Rabbit-shaped Almond Cookies

Ingredients for making Rabbit-shaped Almond Cookies in an oil-free fryer

- Butter 50 g
- Powdered sugar 40 g
- All-purpose flour 100 g
- Egg yolk 1 pc
- Almonds 12 nuts
- Olive oil 1/4 teaspoon

Implementation tools
Oil-free fryer, bowl, mixer

How to make Rabbit-shaped Almond Cookies in an oil-free fryer

1.Mix cake dough
Put in a bowl 50g butter (to soften but not melt), 40g powdered sugar and mix well.

Then, add 1 egg yolk, 100g of flour and continue to mix until the dough forms a smooth, flexible mass.

2.Shaping the cake
Place the dough in between 2 sheets of parchment paper and then roll out the dough to a thickness of about 3mm.

Use a mold to shape, then cover the dough with parchment paper and place in the freezer for 15 minutes.

3.Baking cake
Preheat oven to 175 degrees Celsius for 5 minutes.

Mix 12 almonds with 1/4 teaspoon olive oil. Then pour into a tray and bake for 15 minutes in an air fryer at 175 degrees Celsius.

Place the almonds on the cake and put it in the oven for 15 minutes at 175 degrees Celsius.

4.Finished product
Almond cookies after baking have a beautiful golden brown color, each piece of crispy, fatty and sweet cake mixed with the flesh of almonds is really delicious.

Pineapple Sponge Cake

Besides the usual sponge cake, you can combine with fragrant, sweet and sour pineapple and then bake it in an extremely convenient oil-free fryer. The beautiful golden pineapple cake, spongy and fragrant with a very strange pineapple scent, is very suitable for you to show off your talents in those family parties.

Ingredients for Pineapple Cake

- Pineapple 1 fruit
- Butter 120 gr
- Sugar 170 gr
- 2 eggs
- Wheat flour 200 gr
- Cornstarch 20 gr
- Fresh milk 125 ml
- Cream tartar powder 1/2 tbsp

Tips to choose good pineapple

Color: Choose pineapples with an even yellow color. If the pineapple is too green, the pineapple is not ripe, the sweetness will not be high.
Shape: Choosing round, short pineapples will be more fleshy than oblong ones.
Feel with your hands: Use your hands to gently press the pineapple body, choosing pineapples that are not too soft or too hard.

Pineapple eyes: Choose to buy fruits with large and sparse pineapple eyes, which proves that the pineapple is ripe naturally, not soaked in medicine.

Fragrance: Choose pineapples that are fragrant, do not choose pineapples that are unripe because they are unripe or have a slightly sour smell in a fermented way because these are overripe pineapples.
Pineapple tops: Choose pineapples with fresh green tops, do not choose fruits with dry, wilted, brown tops.

Implementation tools
Air fryer, knife, pot, cup

How to make Pineapple Cake

1.Preparing pineapple

Pineapple cut off the top of the pineapple and peel it around. After peeling, you skillfully use a knife to remove the pineapple eyes and cut into thin circles, removing the middle core.

2.Cooking caramel

Put a pan on the stove, add 60g of sugar, a little water, 1 teaspoon of lemon juice.

Stir over low heat until the sugar is completely dissolved. When the sugar starts to boil, shake the pan until the mixture turns brown, then turn off the heat. Pour caramel into each mold.

3.Mix the egg yolk mixture
Eggs separate yolks and whites. Put in a bowl 2 egg yolks, 120g butter, 20g cornstarch, 200g flour, 125ml fresh milk and 50g sugar and mix well.

4. Whip the egg whites
The egg whites are put in a bowl with 35g of sugar, then beat with a mixer at low speed, lightly beat by hand.

When you see the mixture is milky white, smooth, thick, lift the whisk to see that the eggs form a standing top, turn the bowl upside down to see that the eggs do not fall.

5.Mix cake batter with egg whites
Next, add the yolk mixture earlier into the white mixture and fold gently and evenly.

6.Pour the mold and bake the cake
Arrange pineapple in each fragrant layer in the mold and then pour in the caramel layer. Then pour the cake mixture on top.

Preheat the air fryer to 125 degrees for 5 minutes.

Then bake the cake 3 times, the first time at 140 degrees Celsius for the first 20 minutes, the second time at 150 degrees Celsius for 15 minutes and the last time at 160 degrees Celsius for 10 minutes.

7.Finished product
So there is a delicious pineapple cake right away, the golden color of pineapple with sweet and sour taste, so attractive, isn't it?

Danisa Cookies

Now you can make them every time you crave them at home with an oil-free fryer. The cakes are made elaborately, fragrant with buttermilk as delicious as the ones in the box, while eating the cake while sipping a little hot tea is really wonderful.

Ingredients for making Danisa cookies with an oil-free fryer

- All-purpose flour 120 gr
- Unsalted Butter 90 gr
- Egg white 1 g
- Powdered sugar 50 gr
- (or fine granulated sugar)
- Raisins 50 gr
- Tools: Air fryer, bowl, spoon, egg beater, ...

How to make Danisa cookies in an oil-free fryer

1. Beat the butter mixture

You put unsalted butter in a bowl, mash it and then add the egg whites and stir well before adding powdered sugar. Whisk the flour mixture until the sugar is completely dissolved.

Tip: You can add 1/2 teaspoon of vanilla and a little salt to the flour mixture, making the cake more flavorful.

2.Mix cookie dough
Sift the prepared flour into the flour mixture, then continue to mix until the dough is smooth.

Tip: The amount of flour should be divided appropriately, avoid adding at the same time because it is easy to make the dough clump and affect the quality of the baked goods.

3. Shape the cake
First, you need to spread parchment paper (or foil) on the griddle of the air fryer. Then, you scoop the flour mixture into the ice cream catcher.

Finally, you shape the cookie on the stencil by drawing a circle with the diameter of the cake.

Tip:
If you don't have an ice cream maker, you can roll the dough, then proceed to cut the slices to taste.
If you want the cookies to look appealing, you can place them in the center of the cake and add raisins, crushed almonds or any other nuts you like before baking.

4.Baking cake
Bake the cake at 140 degrees Celsius for 12 minutes, then use chopsticks to turn the other side of the cake and continue to bake at 160 degrees Celsius for another 5 minutes to complete.

5.Finished product

Cookies made with an air fryer still achieve the crispness and beautiful golden color that is like using the oven! Biscuits are one of the favorite snacks of any age, especially when sipping cookies with hot tea is nothing better.
Tips for making a successful cookie:

The temperature of the air fryer can vary between brands, so use a thermometer to measure the temperature in the pot before baking. This helps the cake to cook evenly and have a nice color. It is possible to separate the right amount of flour when mixing with the butter mixture, avoid adding at the same time because it makes the dough easy to clump, difficult to beat and even affects the quality of the cake.
Separate the egg whites carefully, avoiding the yolks to stick, because it is easy to make the cake taste strange.

Baked Banana Cake

Not only have pure baked banana cake, but now you can make delicious and nutritious baked banana cakes combined with almonds and yogurt in an oil-free fryer that couldn't be simpler.

The cake is not difficult to bake but the result is delicious from the table, the cakes will definitely be a very suitable dessert for you to treat your family after each meal.

Ingredients for making Almond Banana Cake with an oil-free fryer

- Ripe banana 400g
- (about 3 fruits)
- Wheat flour 100 g
- Butter 40 g
- Almond flour 50 g
- Sugar 50 g
- 1 egg
- Vanilla sugar 8 g
- Cinnamon powder 1 teaspoon
- Baking powder 4 g
- Salt 1/4 teaspoon
- Sliced almonds 20 gr

Implementation tools
Oil-free fryer, bowl, mixer

How to make Almond Banana Cake with an oil-free fryer

1. Crush bananas
Peel the banana, then put it in a bowl and mash it with a fork.

Pro tip: If you want to use bananas to decorate the cake, leave about half a banana and slice it into 13 pieces!

2.Mix cake dough
Put in a bowl of bananas 40g melted butter, 1 egg, 50g sugar, 1/4 teaspoon salt, then mix well with a spatula.

Add 1 teaspoon of cinnamon powder, 100g of flour, 4g of baking powder, 20g of almonds, 8g of vanilla sugar and continue to mix.

3. Molding
Brush butter around the sides of the pan, line with parchment paper, then pour in the batter.

Arrange sliced banana on top of cake.

4.Baking almond banana cake in an oil-free fryer
Preheat the air fryer first at 160 degrees Celsius for 10 minutes, then add about 50ml of water and bake the cake for 20 minutes.

After 20 minutes, you lower the baking temperature to 150 degrees Celsius and the last 10 minutes bake at 140 degrees Celsius.

5.Finished product

After the cake is done baking, remember to sprinkle more almonds to make the cake more attractive!

The finished banana cake is fragrant, soft and smooth, with the natural sweetness of ripe bananas and the flesh of crispy almonds.

How to store almond banana cake?

You put the cake in an airtight container or covered with food wrap to avoid drying the cake, store it in the refrigerator and use it for 1-2 days to keep the deliciousness of the cake!

Buttermilk Bread

The sweet smell of buttermilk permeates the kitchen, the beautiful little breads made at home in an oil-free fryer are simple and delicious.

The cake remains soft, chewy and fragrant after baking, the sweet and fatty taste of the typical buttermilk will make you feel hungry just by smelling it.

Ingredients for making Buttermilk Bread with an oil-free fryer

- All-purpose flour 300 gr
- Fresh milk without sugar 60 ml
- Unsalted Butter 50 gr
- Instant yeast 5 gr
- Salt 1/4 teaspoon
- Sugar 2 tablespoons
- 1 chicken egg

Tips for buying ingredients:

Instant yeast, unsalted butter you can easily buy at bakeries selling ingredients or e-commerce sites like Tiki, Lazada, Shopee,... are available.

Implementation tools
Fryer without oil, stencils

How to make Buttermilk Bread with an oil-free fryer

1.Mix cake dough
Put 300g of all-purpose flour and 5g of yeast in a bowl, mix well.

Note about yeast:

Put the salt and yeast at a distance from each other, if the yeast comes into direct contact with the salt, the yeast will die.
Tips to check if yeast is still active or not: If yeast is not stored properly, it may weaken or die, to check if your yeast is still active or not, put it in a cup of warm water. . After about 5 minutes, when you see the enamel bubbling up a lot on the surface of the water, your yeast is still good to use.
Add 1/4 teaspoon of salt, 2 tablespoons of sugar, add 1 egg and 60ml of fresh milk.

Mix well.

2.Kneading the dough
Take the dough out and start kneading the dough. First you fold the dough, then use the back of your hand, press and rub, push the dough away (Folding and Stretching). Note that pressing and spreading the dough away, not down. Rotate the dough 90 degrees, repeat the two steps above.

After kneading for 10-15 minutes, the dough becomes chewy and smooth, add 50g of unsalted butter and dried cranberries and knead in the same way and slowly increase the speed of the dough.

Knead until the butter is incorporated into the dough, the dough becomes soft, chewy, smooth and does not stick to your hands. Break the dough out and pull it into a thin film.

Small tips:

If the dough is a bit dry, you can slowly add a little unsweetened fresh milk!

3.Incubate the dough
Cover the bowl with cling film or a thin cloth and let the dough rise for about 45 minutes, depending on room temperature, for the dough to double in size.

4.Dividing and rolling the dough
Sprinkle a little dry flour on the table, put the kneaded dough with the back of your hand, press and rub, push the dough away (Folding and Stretching). Note that pressing and spreading the dough away, not down. Rotate the dough 90 degrees, repeat the two steps above.

Divide the dough into equal portions according to the size of your pan. Cover the dough and let it rest for about 10 minutes before shaping.

5.Shaping the cake and brewing for the 2nd time
Cakes you can mold into circles, spirals or as long as you like.

Cover the dough and let it rest for about 15 minutes before baking.

Note:

Cover the unrolled dough with a towel or food wrap to prevent the dough from drying out.
Do not be too strong when shaping the cake because it will lose the baking ability of the cake when baking, it will lose its deliciousness.

6. Bake the cake with an oil-free fryer
Line a sheet of foil in the tray of the air fryer, heat the pot at 160 degrees for about 4 minutes

Place the cake in the pan. Bake the cake at about 160 degrees Celsius for 5 minutes, then open the pot, turn the cake and bake for about 5 more minutes until the cake is cooked evenly.

7.Finished product
Buttermilk bread is fragrant, sweet, soft and delicious with a unique buttery smell, isn't it? Let's enjoy now!

Sweet Potato Cake

It sounds strange but delicious is the baked sweet potato cake, more especially, the cake is baked in an oil-free fryer, not an oven as usual! In addition to the traditional baked sweet potato cakes, you can also combine coconut milk or create a beautiful stick shape, making the already delicious cake even more delicious.

Ingredients for making Coconut Milk Sweet Potato Cake

- Sweet potato 180 grams
- Oatmeal 120 grams
- 100 grams peanut butter
- Unsweetened coconut milk 60 ml
- Baking powder 1 teaspoon
- (baking soda)
- Sesame seeds 2 teaspoons
- Tools: air fryer, bowl, spoon,...

Tips for choosing delicious sweet potatoes

Choose potatoes with a round or elongated shape, without waist, hollow, slightly squeezed, not too hard; These tubers are usually low in fiber, high in flour and very sweet to eat.
If you want to buy soft, fragrant, and rotten sweet potatoes, you should choose tubers with a layer of chalk or soil attached to them. When slicing a thin slice at the tip of the potato, you will see a light orange color and melt the sap.

If you want to buy flexible sweet potatoes, you should choose purple-red sweet potatoes with bile stains on the skin. When slicing a thin slice at the tip of the potato, it will be light yellow and plastic.

How to make Coconut Milk Sweet Potato Cake

1.Preparing sweet potato
Put the sweet potatoes in a pot of boiling water (it takes about 15-20 minutes) then take them out and let them cool.

Next, peel off the skin, cut it into circles with a knife, and then crush it with a spoon.

See also: How to boil sweet potatoes in the microwave without water

2.Mix the dough
In turn, put 120g of oatmeal, 180g of mashed sweet potato, 100g of peanut butter, 60ml of coconut milk in a bowl and mix well.

Add 1 teaspoon of baking powder to the mixture and gently mix with your hands until the ingredients are combined to form a smooth dough.

3. Shape the cake

Place the dough on a flat surface, roll the dough into a cylinder, and then use a knife to cut into circles. Use your hands to round and flatten the doughnut shape.

Roll the shaped cake over with a layer of sesame seeds for extra appeal. So the cake shaping is done. Repeat until all ingredients are prepared.

4.Baking cake

Turn on the air fryer 10 minutes before at 160 degrees Celsius to stabilize the heat.

Put the cake in an oil-free fryer and bake at 160 degrees Celsius for about 15 minutes. About 10 minutes turn the cake once so that both sides are cooked evenly.

See more: 9 tips for using an oil-free fryer, housewives need to pay attention

5.Finished product

Coconut milk sweet potato cake after completion will have a light brown color, delicious flesh.

So with just a few steps and simple ingredients, you've got fragrant sweet potato cakes mixed with the fat of coconut milk and roasted sesame.

Cakes can be used for breakfast or snacks. Let's try it now and treat the whole family!

Biscotti

For followers of a "clean" diet, an oil-free fryer is an extremely effective assistant. Now you are no longer sad because the air fryer can help you bake delicious and nutritious biscotti in a snap.

Fragrant Biscotti cake, 1 bite crunchy, sweet taste mixed with crunchy, nutritious nuts, it's worth trying at home.

Ingredients for making Green Tea Biscotti in an oil-free fryer

- Oatmeal 120 gr
- All-purpose flour 80 gr
- Matcha powder 8 gr
- Baking soda 3 gr
- Mixed nuts 80 gr
- 1 chicken egg
- Vanilla essence 1/2 teaspoon
- Honey 30 ml
- Olive oil 20 ml
- Lemon juice 1/2 teaspoon
- Diet sugar 20 gr
- 1 pinch salt

What is Oatmeal? Where do you buy it?

Oatmeal or oatmeal is a food made from oat seeds - a whole grain containing many nutritional values.

To make this powder, people take the oat kernels to separate the shell, then use the method of rolling or grinding them to produce a type of oatmeal that has the same nutritional content as the ingredients used to make it.
You can find oatmeal at grocery stores, supermarkets or online on e-commerce sites.

How to distinguish matcha powder and green tea powder?

Matcha powder is a fine powder made from 100% young buds of the green tea plant. This powder is different from green tea powder in terms of nutritional value as well as price, because green tea powder is only ground from 30% of young tea buds and the rest is 70% of young tea leaves.

Matcha powder has a bright green color and has a bitter after-sweet taste that is different from green tea powder, which is dark green, can be slightly yellow and has a bitter taste.
See details: How to distinguish green tea powder and matcha powder

Implementation tools
Air fryer, egg beater, bowl, spoon, knife, sieve, foil, food wrap,...

How to make Green Tea Biscotti in an oil-free fryer

1.Mix dry mixture
First, you mix 80g of the seed mixture with about 10g of oatmeal.

Tip: This mixing will help the particles adhere to the dough better.
Next, take another bowl and then sift in 110g of oatmeal, 80g of flour, 8g of matcha powder, 3g of baking soda and mix well.

2.Mix wet mixture
Separate the yolks and egg whites into 2 separate bowls.

Then, add a little salt to the egg whites and then use a mixer on low speed until the eggs are foamy like soap.

Next, you add 1/2 teaspoon of lemon juice, 20g of sugar and continue to beat at high speed until the egg is slightly thickened, creating a light peak.

Finally, add to the bowl 1/2 teaspoon of vanilla essence, 1 yolk and then use a mixer on low speed for the mixture to blend.

3.Mix dry and wet mixtures
Slowly pour the dry flour, 20ml olive oil, 30ml honey into the beaten egg and mix until the powder is completely dissolved.

Next, you add the dry seed mixture to the flour bowl and mix again until the mixture is evenly combined.

4. Bake the cake for the 1st time
Preheat the air fryer for 5 minutes at 200 degrees Celsius.

Spread the dough into a rectangle evenly on a sheet of foil with a thickness of about 1cm. Then, you bake this dough for the first time for 15 minutes at 150 degrees Celsius.

After 15 minutes, let the dough cool for about 10 minutes, cover with cling film and place in the refrigerator for at least 3 hours.

5. Bake the cake for the 2nd time
Next, cut the dough into thin slices 1cm thick and then bake for a second time for 5 minutes at 150 degrees Celsius.

Finally, turn the cake over and bake a third time for another 5 minutes at 150 degrees Celsius.

Note: Because the cake has been cut into thin slices, it is necessary to adjust the baking temperature accordingly, to avoid burning the cake.

6.Finished product
Green tea biscotti by air fryer has light green color and attractive aroma. Crispy, sweet and greasy cake from nuts, this is definitely a snack to eat

Whole Wheat Bread

If you are in the process of dieting, try making delicious wholemeal bread from your own air fryer at home. Whole grain bread baked in an oil-free fryer is soft and spongy, chewy, chewy, flavorful, served with delicious fruit jam!

Ingredients for making Whole Wheat Bread with an oil-free fryer

- Whole wheat flour 250 gr
- Instant yeast 3 gr
- Water 170 ml
- Cooking oil 10 ml
- Salt 1/2 teaspoon

Implementation tools
Air fryer, bowl, mixer, round cake mold with diameter 16-18cm,...

How to cook Whole Wheat Bread in an oil-free fryer

1.Mix cake dough
Put in a bowl 250g whole wheat flour, 1/2 teaspoon salt and mix well.

Then, add 3g of instant yeast, 10ml of cooking oil, 110ml of water and continue to mix until the dough is sticky.

2.Kneading the dough
Put the dough on the table and knead according to the Folding and Strectching technique.

First, you fold the dough, then use the back of the table to press and spread the dough away. Note that pressing and spreading the dough away, not down. Next, rotate the dough at an angle of 90 degrees and repeat the two steps above for about 15 minutes.

When the dough becomes a smooth, non-sticky mass, press your fingers to have elasticity.

How to identify satisfactory powder:

The powder is smooth, with good elasticity.
The dough does not stick to your hands: When pressed, it feels a bit sticky, but when you lift your fingers, the dough does not stick to your hands.
The dough can be stretched into a thin film without tearing.
Check the dough with Windowpane. Break off part of the dough, stretch it out. If the powder forms a thin film, it is not easy to tear the light can pass through.

3.Incubate the dough

Place dough in a bowl and cover with cling film for 40 minutes - 2 hours (depending on room temperature) until dough has doubled in size.

Tip to identify the dough: Use your hands to press deeply into the dough, if the dough still has an indentation, it means that it has been brewed.

4. Shape the cake
Knead the dough for 1 minute, roll it up and place it in a baking sheet lined with parchment paper. Cover the mold with cling film and incubate a second time for 40 minutes - 2 hours until the dough has doubled in size.

Use a knife to cut 3 short lines, spread a thin layer of water and then sprinkle black sesame, white sesame on the surface of the cake.

5.Baking cake
Preheat the fryer at 150 degrees Celsius for 5 minutes.

Then, put the cake into the fryer and bake at a temperature of 140 degrees C until the surface is golden brown (time ranges from 20 - 40 minutes depending on the capacity of the fryer).

6.Finished product
Whole grain bread baked in an oil-free fryer is soft and spongy, chewy, chewy, delicious, served with delicious fruit jam!

Crab Bread

To make your breakfast more delicious and full of energy, try making crab bread at home with an air fryer.

The finished crab bread has an eye-catching brown crust, the inside is soft and delicious, the smell of the cake is fragrant and smooth, making everyone in the family love it.

Ingredients for making Crab Bread with an oil-free fryer

- All-purpose flour 250 gr
- Light butter 10 gr
- Yeast 5 gr
- 1 chicken egg
- Sugar 3 tbsp
- Milk 10 ml
- Salt 1 teaspoon

Implementation tools
Fryer without oil, stencils,...

How to make Crab Bread with an oil-free fryer

1.Mix cake dough
You need to put the flour in a bowl and then add 1/4 teaspoon of salt, yeast and mix well.

2.Knead the dough
You continue to add unsalted butter and fresh milk and knead until the dough is soft and smooth.

3.Incubate the dough
Put the flour in a large bowl and let it rest for 30-40 minutes.

4.Kneading and rolling the dough
The flour has risen and risen, knead the dough to remove air and divide the dough into equal parts.

Continue to shape each dough block by rolling the dough into a long cylinder. Note that you roll around so that you can create a large cylindrical block and a small cylindrical block as shown below.

Then you roll out the thin dough to about 0.2 cm.

5.Shaping the cake and brewing for the 2nd time
Use a knife to cut the large end of the rolled dough in half. Fold the 2 ends of the dough just cut out to the sides and slowly roll the whole piece of dough to create a crab bread shape.

Finally, you glue the 2 ends of the dough together to complete the crab bread shape.

After shaping the bread, continue to incubate the crab bread for 30-40 minutes.

6. Bake the cake with an oil-free fryer
Line the bottom of the air fryer with parchment paper and place the cooked crab bread into the pot.

Chicken eggs you put in a bowl, beat well and then use a brush to spread the eggs evenly on the surface of the crab bread so that after baking, the bread has a beautiful color.

You continue to bake the cake with an air fryer for 15 minutes at a temperature of 115 degrees Celsius.

7.Finished product
Crab bread after completion has an eye-catching brown crust, soft and delicious inside. This bread is very suitable for breakfast with your family.

Flan

The flan cake is made by air-frying, after finishing, it is smooth, lightly fragrant with vanilla and has the sweet and fatty taste of custard.

The cake will be more delicious when you eat it with black coffee and shaved ice!

Ingredients for making flan with an oil-free fryer

- Chicken eggs 6 eggs
- Fresh milk with sugar 400 ml
- Condensed milk 120 ml
- Sugar 60 g
- Lemon juice 1 teaspoon
- Vanilla 2 tubes

Implementation tools
Fryer without oil

How to cook flan with an oil-free fryer

1.Cooking Caramel
Put a pan on the stove, add 60g of sugar, a little water, 1 teaspoon of lemon juice.

Stir over low heat until the sugar is completely dissolved. When the sugar starts to boil, shake the pan until the mixture turns brown, then turn off the heat.

Note:

You don't need to add too much water, just wet the sugar. When the caramel is finished cooking, quickly pour a thin layer into each cake mold. Avoid keeping for a long time because caramel is easy to solidify when cooled.

2.Mix egg and milk mixture
Put 3 eggs, 3 egg yolks, 400ml fresh milk, 120ml condensed milk in a bowl, stir in one direction with a spatula to blend.

3.Sieve the milk mixture
Strain the milk mixture through a sieve until smooth.

4.Pour the mold and bake the cake
Preheat the air fryer for 10 minutes at 110 degrees Celsius.

Pour the mixture into each cake mold, then bake for 35 minutes at 110 degrees Celsius.

Finally, put the flan in the refrigerator for at least 4 hours before serving.

\

Note: To know if the cake is done, you can use a toothpick to poke the cake and then pull it out. If the toothpick comes out clean, the cake is done, if the mixture is still sticky, the cake is not done.

5.Finished product
The finished flan is smooth, lightly scented with vanilla and has the sweet and fatty taste of custard. The cake will be more delicious when you eat it with black coffee and shaved ice!
12.Cheese cake

If you are a cake lover, you definitely should not miss the cheese cake made with an extremely convenient air fryer. The cake is soft, fragrant with the smell of cheese, and the light fat thanks to the egg butter is very attractive. With each light touch, the cake is so lovely that you can only look at it but don't want to eat it.

Cheese Cake

Ingredients for making Cheese Cake with an oil-free fryer

- Cream cheese 110 gr
- (cream cheese at room temperature)
- Unsalted Butter 70 gr
- Chicken eggs 4 eggs
- All-purpose flour 100 gr
- Sugar 50 gr

Ingredients for cheese sponge cake in an oil-free fryer

Implementation tools:
Oil-free fryer, bowl,...

How to cook Cheesecake in an oil-free fryer
1. Melt the cheese
Put in a pan 110g cream cheese (cream cheese) at room temperature, 70g unsalted butter.

Turn on the low heat, cook and stir until the mixture melts and blends together, then let the mixture cool completely.

2.Mix cake dough
Separate the whites and yolks of 4 eggs.

Place melted and completely cooled cheese and butter in a large bowl, add 4 egg yolks, and mix well.

Add 100g of all-purpose flour, into the bowl of the mixture above, mix to combine.

3. Whip the egg whites
Place 4 egg whites in a large bowl.

Use an electric mixer to beat on low speed until the eggs are foamy like soap.

When large bubbles appear, add about 20g of sugar, beat on low until the sugar dissolves. After 30 seconds of beating, you add about 20g and continue to beat at slow speed.

When adding the last 10g of sugar to the egg bowl, beat at high speed, beat until the eggs are soft, creamy, the mixture is flexible, glossy and smooth, with soft peaks, then lower the speed for another 1-2 minutes. . Lift down the spire to make it.

Tip: You should divide the sugar into 2-3 parts and then beat in turn with the eggs to dissolve the sugar more evenly.

4.Mix egg whites with cake flour
Add the beaten egg whites in small portions to the flour, stirring gently until all the egg whites are used up.

Mix the ingredients together, so you should mix Fold gently (mixing style and flipping from the bottom of the bowl to the top in one direction) and do not mix too hard to avoid breaking a lot of air bubbles that will not bloom well. Mix only until the flour is evenly incorporated into the egg mixture.

Small tips:

You divide the beaten eggs into small pieces and add several times to make the mixture more even.
Folding the dough will help keep the air bubbles, helping to prevent over-swiping that causes water separation for the eggs. In addition, when mixing the flour, it also helps the dough to be less clumpy, and mixes faster and more evenly. If you want to make cakes that use egg whites to help the cake rise, you need to fold the cake gently.
Tip for those who don't know how to fold, you can use a spatula to gently stir in one direction to reduce air bubbles.

5.Pour the mold and bake the cake
Line the cake pan with non-stick baking paper (you can customize it according to your own mold).

Gently pour the flour mixture into the mold, spreading the dough evenly. Gently pat the bottom of the mold to break up any large air bubbles. Wrap a piece of foil on the face of the mold as shown.

Preheat the oven for 10 minutes before baking to 350 degrees F. Bake at 350 degrees F for 10 minutes and lower to 300 degrees F, bake for another 20 minutes until fully cooked.

6.Finished product
Cheese cake with an oil-free fryer is extremely easy to make but delicious with the fatty flavor of cheese, the soft and fluffy cake layer is so attractive. Let's enjoy now!

Egg Tarts

Ingredients for making egg tarts with an oil-free fryer

- 10 pcs egg tart base
- Chicken eggs 2
- Fresh milk without sugar 150 ml
- Condensed milk 3 tablespoons

How to choose and buy fresh ingredients
How to choose to buy fresh chicken eggs

Eggshell: Should choose eggs with a thin layer of white chalk on the outside, feeling rough or heavy to the touch because these are new eggs. If the eggshell is smooth, bright or has cracks, the eggs are not good for a long time.

Examination: When looking at chicken eggs under the light, if the air chamber is small, the yolk is round, does not move, and the white is transparent with a red orange or light pink color, it is a fresh egg. In contrast, older eggs will be red with many ridges around the cell and large air chamber voids.

Shake gently: Hold the egg to your ear and shake it gently, if there is a sound, it is an old egg, for a long time. If you don't listen, but shake the eggs and see the strong movement, the eggs are broken, the chickens are incubating, ...

See details: How to choose to buy fresh and quality chicken eggs
Where to buy egg tart base?

You can buy egg tart base at baking supply stores, large supermarkets or buy on e-commerce sites. When buying, remember to carefully check the expiration date and packaging of the product to ensure safety!

See also: How to make delicious crispy tart shell at home
Ingredients for egg tarts in an oil-free fryer

Implementation tools
Oil-free fryer, pot, bowl, mixer, sieve,...

How to make Egg tarts with an oil-free fryer
1.Make custard mixture
Put the pot on the stove, add 150ml of unsweetened fresh milk, 3 tablespoons of condensed milk. Stir over medium heat for about 3 minutes until the milk mixture is warm and fuming, then turn off the heat.

Outward remittance:

In order for the milk not to be degraded and lose nutrients, you should not boil the milk, just boil it to a warm level!
For those of you who like to eat sweeter, you can increase the amount of condensed milk depending on your taste.

Beat 2 eggs, then slowly add the eggs to the milk mixture, stirring constantly until well combined.

Next, strain the custard mixture through a sieve to make the tart filling smooth.

2.Make egg tarts
Preheat the air fryer to 200 degrees Celsius for 5 minutes.

Next, place the tart bases inside the pot and bake at 180 degrees C for 4 minutes.

Then, you pour the custard mixture into each tart base and continue to bake for another 7 minutes at 180 degrees Celsius to complete.

Repeat with the rest of the batches until you run out of ingredients.

3.Finished product
Egg tarts are made in an oil-free fryer with a crispy crust, fragrant butter aroma combined with smooth egg cream filling, fatty leopard and moderate sweetness, so eating without feeling bored.

Cat Tongue Cake

Ingredients for Cat Tongue Cake

- All-purpose flour 130 gr
- 100 gr . unsalted butter
- Powdered sugar 110 gr
- Egg white 1 pc
- Vanilla essence 1 ml

Implementation tools
Air fryer, bowl, spoon, stencils, ice cream bag,...

How to make Traditional Cat Tongue Cake

1.Mix butter and sugar
Put in a bowl 100g soft unsalted butter (not melted), 110g powdered sugar. Use a spatula to mix well until combined.

Add about 1ml vanilla, 1 egg white and continue to mix.

Note: You should not add a lot of vanilla because it will make the cake bitter.
Step 1 Mix butter and sugar Traditional cat tongue cakeStep 1 Beat butter and sugar Traditional cat tongue cake
2.Mix cake dough
Divide the dough into 3 parts, add each part in turn to the butter and sugar mixture and mix until the mixture is smooth. Then let the dough rest for 10 minutes.

3.Shaping a cat's tongue
Line a plate with parchment paper and then begin to shape the cake.

Put the flour mixture into the ice cream bag, squeeze the cream into pieces about 3 knuckles long. Remember to leave a little distance, because the cake will expand when it's cooked.

4. Bake the cake with an oil-free fryer
Preheat the air fryer at 180 degrees Celsius for 10 minutes, then bake the cakes at 170 degrees Celsius for 15 minutes.

5.Finished product
Cat tongue cake has a beautiful golden brown color, with a slight smell of butter, when eaten, the cake is crispy with sweet and fatty taste, extremely delicious.

Pumpkin Cake

Pumpkin Cake Ingredients

- Pumpkin 150 gr
- All-purpose flour 250 gr
- Fresh milk 30 ml
- (no sugar)
- Yeast blooms 4 gr
- 1 egg
- Butter 1 tbsp
- Sugar 1 tbsp
- Vanilla extract 1 teaspoon

Implementation tools
Air fryer, bowl, cup, pot, food wrap,...

How to make Pumpkin Cake

1.Steaming and addicted to squash
Peel the pumpkin, then cut it into small pieces. Then steam for about 10 minutes until the squash is cooked.

After the pumpkin is steamed, put it in a bowl and mash it.

Tip for fast and smooth squash mash: Take a strainer to place on a bowl, put the pumpkin on the sieve, and then use a spoon to mash and press down to let the squash pass through the sieve. .

The part of squash that passes through the sieve is small, smooth and even.

2.Mix cake dough

You break 1 egg into the bowl of mashed squash, then mix them well, then add 1 tablespoon of sugar, 30ml of unsweetened fresh milk, 1 tablespoon of butter, 1/3 teaspoon of salt, 1 teaspoon of extract vanilla, continue to mix well again.

Next, you put 4g of yeast in the bowl of pumpkin mixture, mix well. Continue to sift 250g of flour into the bowl of squash mixture.

Finally, you mix everything together and the powder absorbs all the water.

Note: To prevent the dough from clumps, you should divide the flour into several times to sift into the bowl of mashed squash because doing so will absorb the water evenly.

3. Kneading the dough

After the dough has absorbed all the water, use your hands to knead the dough thoroughly until the dough is flexible.

4.Incubate the dough

When the dough is flexible and no longer sticks to the bowl, cover the bowl with cling film and let the dough rest for about 2 minutes.

After 20 minutes of incubating the dough, take the dough out and knead it again for about 1 minute to make it flexible.

5.Shaping the pumpkin
The dough has been incubated for enough time, you divide the dough evenly into 4 small dough blocks. Then roll each dough ball and shape it into a squash shape.

Method 1: Create a shape by cutting a wedge shape

You rub the dry powder into the palm of your hand to prevent sticking, then use your hands to gently press the dough to make it more beautiful.

Rub the tip of the scissors in cooking oil to prevent sticking and make cutting easier, then use scissors to create a petal shape.

Method 2: Column seconds

Use a thin and small string to tie around the dough to divide it into 8 packs as shown.

Note:

Do not tie too tightly because the dough will continue to expand quite large when the second incubation and baking.

6. Baking bread

You use a brush to brush a thin layer of oil on the cakes, so that when baking the cake is more beautiful.

Then, you heat the air fryer for about 5 minutes at 180 degrees. Next, put the shaped pumpkin cake in an oil-free fryer, choose 180 degrees, and bake for about 15 minutes.

After 15 minutes, take out the cake to turn it over and bake it again at 180 degrees for 10 minutes to cook evenly on both sides.

7. Finished product

After baking, pumpkin cake looks like a beautiful yellow-orange pumpkin. The outside crust is crispy, the inside is spongy and soft.

The light pastry taste combined with the fatty taste of butter and milk is extremely delicious and attractive, sure to make my whole family compliment it!

Pumpkin Muffins

Ingredients for making Pumpkin Muffins with an oil-free fryer

- Plain Muffin Remix Cake Flour 250 g
- (or all-purpose flour - flour number 11)
- Eggs 150 g
- (3 fruits)
- Milk 150 g
- Cooking oil 170 g
- Pumpkin 240 g
- (remove shell)
- Raisins and cranberries 50 g

How to choose a delicious pumpkin
Choose pumpkins that are heavy, firm, and have smooth skins.
Choose fruit with stalks 2 - 5cm long. Short-stemmed fruits are
more susceptible to rapid rotting.
The fruit is round, naturally notched into relatively even parts.
Delicious squash is usually yellow-orange, mixed with dark
green, yellow in the flesh and has a sweet, aromatic taste and
relative plasticity.
See details:

How to choose to buy delicious pumpkin
The effect of pumpkin
How to store pumpkin?
You wash the pumpkin, then put it in a vacuum bag and store it
in the refrigerator at a temperature of 5-8 degrees Celsius.

If you want to keep it longer, you should put the squash in the freezer with a temperature of -8 to -10 degrees Celsius. When you want to use it for processing, you should defrost the squash in the refrigerator until thawed, do not thaw with water because water will cause the nutrients of the squash to be washed away.

Implementation tools
Oil-free fryer, bowl, mixer

How to make Pumpkin Muffins in an oil-free fryer

1.Steamed and mashed pumpkin
Steam 240g pumpkin, then mash it with a fork.

Pro tip: You can use a blender to blend the squash to make it smoother.

2.Mix cake dough
Put 3 chicken eggs, 150g milk, 170g cooking oil in a bowl, then mix well to combine.

Next, add 250g of flour and mix until the mixture is light yellow and smooth.

Finally add the pumpkin and mix well.

3. Molding
Pour batter into cupcake pan, sprinkle with raisins and blueberries.

4.Baking cake
Preheat the air fryer at 130 degrees Celsius for 5 minutes, then put the cake in the oven for 22 minutes.

5.Finished product
Pumpkin muffin is extremely fluffy, when you eat it, you can feel the sweet, fatty taste of pumpkin, with the slight sour taste of raisin and blueberry topping. Making this cake to entertain the whole family is a great deal!

Contents

Printed in Great Britain
by Amazon

53457444R00077